ROAST CHICKEN AND CURRY SALAD

Don't be deceived by the word "salad" in this dish—it includes all of the basic food groups, making it an excellent (and complete) supper.

INGREDIENTS

Serves 4

Dressing:

½ cup plain yogurt

½ cup mayonnaise

2 tablespoons freshly squeezed lemon juice

2 teaspoons curry powder

1 scallion, chopped

Salt and coarsely ground black pepper

Salad:

12 new potatoes, scrubbed and cut in half

2 large free-range eggs

2 cups broccoli florets, cut small

½ a roast chicken, skinned and cubed

1 small red onion, finely sliced

12 cherry tomatoes, halved

2 Persian cucumbers, sliced diagonally

1 medium red apple, cored and cubed

2 tablespoons coarsely chopped coriander

2 tablespoons coarsely chopped mint

PREPARATION

1. Blend together the yogurt, mayonnaise, lemon juice, and curry powder in a blender until smooth. Add the scallion, and salt and pepper to taste. Transfer to an airtight container and refrigerate until ready to use.

2. Place the potatoes in a large pot and cover with salted water. Bring to a boil and cook until soft, about 20 minutes. Drain and set aside.

3. Place the eggs in a small pot and cover with water. Bring to a boil, reduce heat, and cook for 12 minutes. Run the eggs under cold water to cool. Peel, and cut into quarters.

4. Bring a pot of salted water to a boil. Add the broccoli, and blanch for about 4 minutes. Drain and set aside.

5. Arrange the potatoes, eggs, broccoli, chicken, onion, cherry tomatoes, cucumbers, and apple on a large serving dish. Sprinkle the coriander and mint on top.

6. Drizzle the dressing over the salad, just before serving.

THAI-STYLE GRILLED BEEF SALAD

The chili pepper, ginger, and soy sauce in this dressing make it sweet, spicy, and simply delicious. Serve with steamed white rice for a lovely Southeast Asian meal.

INGREDIENTS

Serves 4

Dressing:

1 cup plain yogurt

1 small red chili pepper, seeded and chopped

2 Persian cucumbers, peeled and seeded

1 scallion, chopped

2 cloves garlic, crushed

1 teaspoon freshly squeezed lime juice

1 tablespoon grated fresh ginger

1 teaspoon sugar

1 teaspoon soy sauce

Salad:

2 pounds beef rump roast, thinly sliced

2 tablespoons sweet chili sauce

2 tablespoons soy sauce

1 clove garlic, crushed

1 tablespoon peanut oil

1 bunch watercress, trimmed

1 scallion, chopped

½ pound snow peas, trimmed and sliced lengthwise

1 carrot, sliced into thin 3-inch sticks

12 cherry tomatoes, halved

1 yellow pepper, thinly sliced lengthwise

PREPARATION

1. Blend together the yogurt, chili pepper, cucumbers, scallion, garlic, lime juice, ginger, sugar, and soy sauce in a blender, until smooth. Transfer to an airtight container and refrigerate until ready to use.

2. Place the beef in a large bowl. Add the chili sauce, soy sauce, and garlic, and toss to coat. Heat the peanut oil in a wok, over medium-high heat. Fry the beef in batches until brown all over, about 5 minutes on each side.

3. Arrange the watercress, scallion, snow peas, carrot, cherry tomatoes, and pepper on a large serving dish, and put layers of beef on top.

4. Drizzle the dressing over the salad, just before serving.

LIGHT AND TANGY POTATO SALAD

Using yogurt instead of mayonnaise makes this dish lighter than most potato salads. Adding sweet potatoes gives it a lovely color.

INGREDIENTS

Serves 4

Dressing:

¼ cup extra virgin olive oil

¼ cup plain yogurt

1 tablespoon freshly squeezed lemon juice

1 teaspoon whole grain mustard

1 clove garlic, crushed

½ teaspoon sea salt

½ teaspoon chopped fresh dill

Salad:

3 medium potatoes, peeled and cut into ½-inch cubes

1 large sweet potato, peeled and cut into ½-inch cubes

Olive oil for roasting

Medium coarse salt

4 ounces arugula, coarsely chopped

2 Persian cucumbers, sliced into rounds

½ small red onion, sliced

1 scallion, sliced diagonally

PREPARATION

1. Blend together the oil, yogurt, lemon juice, mustard, garlic, salt, and dill in a blender until smooth. Transfer to an airtight container and refrigerate until ready to use.

2. Preheat the oven to 400°F. Place the potatoes in a large pot. Cover with salted water and parboil for about 15 minutes. Drain, rinse, and pat dry. Place on a large baking sheet, and coat well with olive oil. Sprinkle with a pinch of salt, and roast for about 20 minutes, or until the potatoes are golden.

3. Transfer the potatoes while hot to a large mixing bowl. Add the arugula, cucumbers, onion, and scallion, and toss. Set aside to cool.

4. Pour dressing on top and mix gently until coated. Transfer to a salad bowl and serve.

SMOKED SALMON AND LIME DIP

Cream cheese and smoked salmon make a perfect brunch-time pair. Serving this dip with freshly toasted bagels and hot coffee provides an excellent incentive for getting out of bed, even on Sunday mornings!

INGREDIENTS

Serves 4

¾ cup plain yogurt

2 teaspoons freshly squeezed lime juice

½ teaspoon freshly grated lime zest

½ tablespoon fresh dill, chopped

¼ teaspoon salt

1 teaspoon sugar

¼ cup smooth cream cheese

½ pound smoked salmon, shredded

PREPARATION

1. Place the yogurt, lime juice, lime zest, dill, salt, sugar, and cream cheese in a medium bowl, and whisk until smooth.

2. Add the salmon, and mix gently until well combined.

3. Transfer to a serving dish, and refrigerate until ready to serve.

SPICY LENTIL DIP

*With its distinct taste of India, this dip is sure to draw plenty of compliments—
and requests for more. Serve with fresh pita or nan.*

INGREDIENTS

Serves 4 to 6

1 tablespoon olive oil

1 tablespoon butter

1 small onion, finely chopped

2 cloves garlic, crushed

1 tablespoon grated fresh
ginger

1 medium tomato, diced

1 small red chili pepper,
seeded and finely chopped

1 teaspoon sugar

½ teaspoon salt

1 teaspoon garam masala

1 cup canned lentils, drained

1½ cups plain yogurt

1 tablespoon chopped fresh
coriander

PREPARATION

1. Heat the olive oil and butter in
a large pan, over medium-high
heat. Add the onion, garlic, and
ginger, and sauté until the onion
turns glassy.

2. Mix in the tomato, chili
pepper, sugar, salt, and garam
masala. Reduce heat, and simmer
for about 10 minutes.

3. Add the lentils, and simmer for
another 5 minutes. Remove from
heat, and set aside to cool.

4. Add the lentils, and simmer for
another 5 minutes. Remove from
heat, and set aside to cool.

GINGER, CARROT, AND CORIANDER DIP

The combination of herbs and spices in this dip is unique, and sure to attract lots of attention on any table of appetizers. Using fresh ginger adds a refreshingly spicy zip.

INGREDIENTS

Serves 4 to 6

1 teaspoon butter

1 teaspoon olive oil

1 small onion, finely chopped

2 small carrots, peeled and diced

1 teaspoon sugar

1 tablespoon grated fresh ginger

¼ teaspoon caraway seeds

¼ teaspoon ground nutmeg

2 cups plain yogurt

2 tablespoons finely chopped coriander

PREPARATION

1. Heat the butter and oil in a saucepan, over medium heat. Add the onion, carrots, sugar, and ginger, and cook over low-medium heat until tender and golden.

2. Crush the caraway seeds with a mortar and pestle. Stir the crushed seeds and the nutmeg into the vegetables. Remove from heat, and set aside to cool.

3. Transfer the carrot mixture to a large glass bowl, and mix in the yogurt and coriander.

4. Cover with plastic wrap, and refrigerate until ready to serve.

ZUCCHINI AND CARROT DIP

Brightly colored and bursting with vitamins, this healthy dip is perfect for serving with oven-baked vegetable chips.

INGREDIENTS

Serves 4

2 tablespoons olive oil

1 medium carrot, peeled and grated

1 medium zucchini, grated

2 cloves garlic, crushed

½ teaspoon sugar

1 scallion, thinly sliced

Salt and freshly ground black pepper

2 cups plain yogurt

1 tablespoon finely chopped fresh mint

1 tablespoon finely chopped fresh basil

PREPARATION

1. Heat the oil in a small saucepan over medium heat. Add the carrot, zucchini, garlic, sugar, scallion, and salt and pepper to taste, and sauté until the vegetables are shiny and tender. Remove from heat, and set aside to cool.

2. Separately, whisk together the yogurt, mint, and basil in a large mixing bowl, until blended.

3. Transfer the yogurt mixture to a serving dish and place the carrot mixture on the top.

4. Cover with plastic wrap, and refrigerate until ready to serve.

ROAST EGGPLANT, FETA, AND MINT SPREAD

Eggplant and feta cheese give this spread a distinct Mediterranean flavor. Serve with freshly toasted pita bread for a light lunch.

INGREDIENTS

Serves 4 to 6

2 large eggplants, cut into 1-inch cubes

Salt

Olive oil, for roasting

1 cup plain yogurt

½ cup crumbled feta cheese

1 tablespoon finely chopped fresh mint

PREPARATION

1. Place the eggplant in a large colander, and sprinkle generously with salt. Set aside for 10 minutes, then pat with a paper towel to remove salt.

2. Preheat the oven to 350°F.

3. Arrange the eggplant on a baking sheet, and coat well with olive oil.

4. Roast for about 40 minutes, or until the eggplant is golden and tender. Remove from the oven, and set aside to cool.

5. In a medium bowl, combine the yogurt, feta, and mint. Gently fold in the eggplant.

6. Transfer to an airtight container, and refrigerate until ready to serve.

TOMATO AND BASIL DIP

Serve this aromatic and colorful dip with toasted pita wedges, for a low-fat alternative to ordinary chips and dip.

INGREDIENTS

Serves 4 to 6

2 cups plain yogurt

4 cocktail or cherry tomatoes, diced

1 scallion, diced

1 clove garlic, crushed

1 tablespoon extra virgin olive oil

¼ teaspoon sugar

2 tablespoons finely chopped fresh basil

Salt and freshly ground black pepper

PREPARATION

1. Place the yogurt, tomatoes, scallion, garlic, oil, sugar, and basil in a large bowl, and whisk together. Add salt and pepper to taste.

2. Transfer to an airtight container, and refrigerate until ready to serve.

SPINACH RAITA

This mild dip is a traditional Indian side dish. Serve it with your favorite spicy curry as a cooling respite for your palate.

INGREDIENTS

Serves 4 to 6

1 pound baby spinach leaves, trimmed

2 cups plain yogurt

2 cloves garlic, crushed

1 tablespoon finely chopped fresh coriander

Salt and freshly ground black pepper

PREPARATION

1. Wash the spinach thoroughly, but do not dry it. Place in a non-stick pot, and cook over medium heat until the spinach wilts. Remove from the heat, and squeeze to remove excess water.

2. Whisk together the yogurt, garlic, coriander, and salt and pepper to taste, in a bowl.

3. Gently stir in the spinach with a large fork, taking care to separate the leaves.

4. Transfer to an airtight container, and refrigerate until ready to serve.

ZUCCHINI, FETA, AND CUMIN DIP

Whole cumin seeds are one of my most treasured spices. Toasting them brings an incredible aroma to my kitchen, and adds a crunchy spiciness to this dip.

INGREDIENTS

Serves 4 to 6

1 teaspoon cumin seeds

1 tablespoon olive oil

1 small onion, finely chopped

1 medium zucchini, diced

Sea salt

¼ teaspoon ground nutmeg

½ cup crumbled feta cheese

2 tablespoons finely chopped fresh coriander

2 cups plain yogurt

Freshly ground black pepper

PREPARATION

1. Toast the cumin seeds in a dry pan over medium heat for about 2 minutes, until aromatic. Set aside.

2. Heat the oil in a saucepan over medium heat. Add the onion, zucchini, and salt to taste, and sauté over low-medium heat for about 10 minutes, until the vegetables are tender and golden.

3. Stir in the cumin, nutmeg, and feta. Remove from the heat, and set aside to cool.

4. Transfer the zucchini mixture to a large glass bowl. Mix in the coriander, yogurt, salt, and pepper to taste.

5. Cover with plastic wrap, and refrigerate until ready to serve.

TZATZIKI

This traditional Greek dish is light and fresh. Serve with salty pretzel sticks or crispy fresh vegetables.

INGREDIENTS

Serves 4 to 6

2 cups plain yogurt

1 English cucumber, peeled and diced

4 teaspoons fresh dill, chopped

4 teaspoons fresh mint, chopped

¼ teaspoon paprika

Salt and freshly ground black pepper

PREPARATION

1. Place the yogurt, cucumber, dill, mint, and paprika in a medium bowl, and whisk together. Add salt and pepper to taste.

2. Transfer to an airtight container, and refrigerate until ready to serve.

COTTAGE CHEESE AND APRICOT SPREAD

Enhance ordinary cottage cheese with apricots and mint. Serve on a toasted baguette for a nutritious alternative to jam or preserves.

INGREDIENTS

Serves 4 to 6

½ cup plain cottage cheese

1½ cups plain yogurt

¼ cup dried apricots, finely diced

1 tablespoon finely chopped fresh mint

2 tablespoons milk

2 tablespoons honey

PREPARATION

1. Place the cottage cheese, yogurt, apricots, mint, and milk in a medium bowl, and mix well.

2. Transfer to an airtight container, and refrigerate for at least 20 minutes, or until ready to serve.

3. Drizzle honey on top, just before serving.

SOUPS

CHILLED CUCUMBER SOUP WITH CURRY RELISH

With a combination of flavors that is both spicy and sweet, this summertime soup is sure to draw requests for seconds! You might want to make a double batch right from the start.

INGREDIENTS

Serves 4

Soup:

2 Persian cucumbers, peeled, seeded, and finely diced

1 Golden Delicious apple, peeled, cored, and finely diced

1¼ cups plain yogurt

⅓ cup water

1 teaspoon salt

⅓ cup milk

Relish:

1 tablespoon vegetable oil

1 small onion, quartered and thinly sliced

1 celery stalk, thinly sliced

1 tablespoon finely chopped fresh coriander

1 teaspoon ground cumin

2 tablespoons coarsely chopped walnuts

1 teaspoon light brown sugar

¼ teaspoon ground turmeric

1 clove garlic, crushed

½ teaspoon red pepper flakes crushed

¼ teaspoon ground ginger

Salt

1 cup frozen peas, thawed

PREPARATION

1. Place the cucumbers, apple, yogurt, water, salt, and milk in a food processor, and process until smooth.

2. Transfer the soup to an airtight container, and refrigerate for at least 1 hour.

3. Heat the oil in a large pan over medium heat. Add the onion, celery, coriander, cumin, walnuts, light brown sugar, turmeric, garlic, red pepper flakes, ginger, and a pinch of salt. Cook while stirring over low heat until the vegetables are tender.

4. Stir in the peas, and cook for a few more minutes. Remove from the heat, and set aside to cool.

5. Transfer the relish to an airtight container, and refrigerate for at least 1 hour.

6. Serve chilled, with a heaping tablespoon of relish on each serving.

CHILLED GINGER AND LIME SOUP

The sublime spiciness in this soup is offset by the yogurt. A perfect chilled soup for people with delicate taste buds.

INGREDIENTS

Serves 4

1 tablespoon butter

2 scallions, finely diced

2 tablespoons grated fresh ginger

2 teaspoons freshly squeezed lime juice

2 teaspoons freshly grated lime zest

2 cloves garlic, crushed

¼ teaspoon crushed red pepper flakes, plus more for garnish

1 teaspoon sugar

Salt

3 cups plain yogurt

1 tablespoon coarsely chopped fresh coriander, plus more for garnish

PREPARATION

1. Heat the butter in a small pan over medium heat. Add the scallions, ginger, lime juice, lime zest, and garlic, and sauté until the scallions turn glassy.

2. Reduce heat, and add the crushed pepper flakes, sugar, and salt to taste. Cook until the sugar has dissolved, then remove from heat, and set aside to cool.

3. Blend with an immersion blender until smooth. Stir in the yogurt and coriander.

4. Transfer to an airtight container, and refrigerate for at least 1 hour.

5. Serve chilled, and garnish with fresh coriander and red pepper flakes.

CHILLED SWEET POTATO AND PEAR SOUP

The aromatic combination of cloves, cinnamon, and nutmeg will fill your kitchen as this soup simmers gently. A delight for all the senses.

INGREDIENTS

Serves 4

1 tablespoon butter

1 small red onion, thinly sliced

3 whole cloves

2 cinnamon sticks

2 whole nutmegs

1 tablespoon light brown sugar

2 large sweet potatoes, peeled and cut into ¼-inch cubes

2 medium Bosc pears, peeled, cored, and diced

2 cups vegetable or chicken stock

Salt and freshly ground black pepper

1 cup plain yogurt

3 sprigs of fresh mint, plus extra for garnish

PREPARATION

1. Heat the butter in a deep pan over medium heat. Add the onion, cloves, cinnamon, nutmegs, and light brown sugar, and sauté until the onion is tender and the sugar has dissolved.

2. Add the sweet potatoes, pears, stock, salt, and pepper to taste, and bring to a boil. Reduce heat and simmer, covered, for about 20 minutes, until the potatoes and pears are soft.

3. Remove from the heat, and set aside to cool. Remove the cloves, cinnamon sticks, and nutmegs. Add the yogurt and mint, and blend with an immersion blender until smooth.

4. Transfer to an airtight container, and refrigerate for at least 1 hour, or until ready to serve.

5. Serve chilled, and garnished with fresh mint.

LEMON AND ZUCCHINI SOUP

With its light texture and delicate taste, this soup makes a lovely first course for any meal.

INGREDIENTS

Serves 4

1 tablespoon olive oil

1 tablespoon butter

2 leeks, finely diced

Sea salt and black pepper

2 pounds zucchini, peeled and diced

2 teaspoons freshly grated lemon zest

2 cups vegetable or chicken stock

1 cup plain yogurt

2 cloves garlic, crushed

1 tablespoon finely chopped fresh parsley

1 tablespoon finely chopped fresh basil

1 cup freshly grated Parmesan cheese

PREPARATION

1. Heat the oil and butter in a large pot over medium heat. Add the leeks, and salt and pepper to taste, and sauté until the leeks are tender.

2. Mix in the zucchini, lemon zest, and stock, and bring to a boil.

3. Reduce heat to low, and simmer for 15 minutes, until the zucchini is soft. Remove from heat, and set aside to cool.

4. Stir in the yogurt, garlic, parsley, basil, and Parmesan cheese.

5. Use a potato masher to break up the zucchini so that the soup has a smoother consistency.

6. Reheat gently on low heat before serving.

SPICY LENTIL SOUP

The variety of spices in this hearty soup will send your taste buds tingling. Serve with freshly baked pumpernickel for a hot lunch on a cold winter day.

INGREDIENTS

Serves 4

1 tablespoon olive oil

1 tablespoon butter

1 small onion, finely diced

Salt

1 teaspoon cumin seeds

1 teaspoon coriander seeds

1 celery stalk, finely diced

1 medium carrot, peeled and grated

2 tablespoons grated fresh ginger

1 clove garlic, crushed

1 teaspoon ground nutmeg

¼ teaspoon ground cinnamon

½ teaspoon crushed red pepper flakes

¼ teaspoon ground turmeric

1 teaspoon soy sauce

1 teaspoon sugar

1 large tomato, diced

1½ cups canned lentils, washed and drained

3½ cups vegetable or chicken stock

2 bay leaves

¾ cup plain yogurt

1 tablespoon finely chopped fresh basil

PREPARATION

1. Heat the oil and butter in a large pot over medium heat. Add the onion and salt to taste, and sauté until the onion turns glassy.

2. Crush the cumin and coriander seeds with a mortar and pestle. Add the celery, carrot, ginger, garlic, nutmeg, cinnamon, pepper flakes, turmeric, and crushed cumin and coriander seeds, and cook over low heat for about 5 minutes.

3. Add the soy sauce, sugar, tomato, lentils, stock, and bay leaves, and bring to a boil. Reduce heat, and simmer until the tomatoes are soft, about 20 minutes.

4. Remove from the heat, and set aside to cool. Remove the bay leaves. Stir in the yogurt and basil.

5. Reheat gently on low heat before serving.

HEARTY BEAN SOUP

With beans, barley, and lots of fresh spinach, this nutritious soup is full of vitamins and minerals. Serve with a chunk of whole grain bread for a satisfying lunch or light supper.

INGREDIENTS

Serves 4

½ pound white kidney beans, soaked overnight

½ pound red kidney beans, soaked overnight

½ cup pearl barley, rinsed and drained

Salt

2 tablespoons extra virgin olive oil

1 leek, finely diced

¾ cup fresh finely chopped fresh flat-leaf parsley

4 cloves garlic, crushed

2 celery stalks, diced

2 medium carrots, peeled and grated

1 can (28-ounce) crushed tomatoes

1 teaspoon sugar

3 cups vegetable or chicken stock

2 cups fresh spinach, finely chopped

Freshly ground black pepper

1 cup plain yogurt

PREPARATION

1. Drain the beans, and rinse in cold water. Place in a large pot, cover with fresh water, and bring to a boil. Reduce heat, and simmer until the beans are soft, about 40 minutes. Rinse with cold water, drain, and set aside.

2. In the meantime, fill a small pot with water and bring to a boil. Add the barley, and salt to taste, and reduce heat to low. Simmer until the barley is tender, about 30 minutes. Rinse with cold water, drain, and set aside.

3. Heat the oil in a large pot over medium heat. Add the leek, and salt to taste, and sauté until tender.

4. Add the parsley, garlic, celery, and carrots. Cook while stirring for 10 minutes, or until the vegetables are tender

5. Mix in the kidney beans, barley, tomatoes, sugar, and stock, and bring to a boil. Reduce heat, and simmer until the vegetables are soft, about 20 minutes.

6. Stir in the spinach, and add salt and pepper to taste. Simmer for another 5 minutes, or until the spinach is tender.

7. Remove from the heat, and set aside to cool. Stir in the yogurt.

8. Reheat gently on low heat before serving.

BROCCOLI, FETA, AND PARMESAN SOUP

Broccoli and cheese are always great companions. In this dish they are joined by a hint of rosemary and a dash of nutmeg, producing a soup that is aromatic and subtly spiced.

INGREDIENTS

Serves 4

4 cups broccoli florets, cut small

Salt

2 cups vegetable or chicken stock

3 sprigs of fresh rosemary

2 teaspoons extra virgin olive oil

2 teaspoons butter

1 small red onion, finely diced

½ teaspoon ground nutmeg

1 teaspoon sugar

½ cup crumbled feta cheese

½ teaspoon freshly ground black pepper

1½ cups plain yogurt

½ cup freshly grated Parmesan cheese, for garnish

PREPARATION

1. Place the broccoli in the basket of a vegetable steamer, and sprinkle with a pinch of salt. Place the stock and rosemary in the bottom of the steamer. Cover the steamer, and bring to a boil. Reduce heat, and just steam until the broccoli is tender, and still bright in color. Discard the rosemary, and set aside the stock.

2. Heat the oil and butter in a large pot over medium heat. Add the onion, nutmeg, and salt to taste, and sauté until tender.

3. Stir in the broccoli. Pour in the stock, and bring to a boil. Reduce heat, and simmer for about 10 minutes.

4. Add the sugar, feta, and pepper, and simmer for about 2 minutes. Remove from the heat, and set aside to cool.

5. Add the yogurt, and blend with an immersion blender until smooth. Do not purée.

6. Reheat gently on low heat before serving. Garnish each bowl with a heaping tablespoon of Parmesan cheese.

GREEN BEAN AND POTATO SOUP

*Green bean soup is a standard favorite in many kitchens. This version is
particularly comforting, thanks to its creamy sweet potatoes.*

INGREDIENTS

Serves 6

1 teaspoon extra virgin olive
oil

1 teaspoon butter

1 small red onion, finely
chopped

2 cloves garlic, minced

1 celery stalk, finely chopped

2 pounds fresh green beans,
trimmed and finely diced

1 large sweet potato, peeled
and finely chopped

1 large potato, peeled and
finely chopped

4 cups vegetable or chicken
stock

Salt and coarsely ground black
pepper

2 tablespoons finely chopped
fresh basil

2 tablespoons finely chopped
fresh marjoram

2 tablespoons finely chopped
fresh mint

1 cup plain yogurt

½ cup freshly grated Parmesan
cheese

PREPARATION

1. Heat the oil and butter in a
large pot. Add the onion, garlic,
and celery, and sauté until the
onion turns glassy.

2. Add the beans, potatoes, 2 cups
of the stock, and salt and pepper
to taste, and bring to a boil.

3. Reduce the heat and simmer
until the vegetables are soft,
about 15 minutes.

4. Mash the potatoes with a
potato masher. Stir in the basil,
marjoram, and mint, and the
remaining 2 cups of the stock.
Simmer for 10 minutes, then
remove from heat and set aside to
cool. Stir in the yogurt and cheese.

5. Reheat gently over low heat,
just before serving.

ROAST PUMPKIN SOUP

Pumpkins aren't just for carving. This dish contains deliciously roasted fresh pumpkin—a perfect soup for celebrating autumn.

INGREDIENTS

Serves 4

3 pounds fresh pumpkin, peeled and cubed

3 tablespoons olive oil

1 teaspoon light brown sugar

1 tablespoon caraway seeds

Salt

1 teaspoon butter

1 small red onion, finely diced

1 medium potato, peeled and cubed

2 cloves garlic, crushed

¼ teaspoon crushed red pepper flakes 1 cup milk

2 bay leaves

2 cups vegetable or chicken stock

1 cup plain yogurt

¼ cup finely chopped fresh parsley

½ cup freshly grated Parmesan cheese, for garnish

PREPARATION

1. Preheat the broiler to 300°F. Arrange the pumpkin pieces on a baking sheet and drizzle 2 tablespoons of the olive oil on top. Sprinkle the light brown sugar, caraway seeds, and salt to taste on the top. Roast until the pumpkin is soft, about 45 minutes.

2. Heat the butter and remaining tablespoon of olive oil in a large pot over a high heat. Add the onion and a pinch of salt, and sauté until tender.

3. Stir in the potato, garlic, and red pepper flakes, and cook over medium heat for a few minutes. Add the milk, bay leaves, and 1 cup of the stock. Reduce heat, and simmer until the potatoes are soft. Remove the bay leaves.

4. Mix in the roasted pumpkin and caraway seeds, and the remaining stock, and simmer for 10 minutes. Remove from heat, and set aside to cool.

5. Blend with an immersion blender until smooth. Stir in the yogurt and parsley.

6. Reheat gently on low heat before serving. Garnish each bowl with a heaping tablespoon of Parmesan cheese.

VEGETABLE BEEF SOUP

Adding yogurt to traditional beef soup makes it creamier than usual. With a variety of spices, this soup is much more interesting than standard fare.

INGREDIENTS

Serves 6

2 pounds beef, cut into ½-inch cubes

1 teaspoon ground cumin

Salt and black pepper

2 tablespoons olive oil

1 tablespoon butter

1 medium red onion, thinly sliced

1 leek, finely diced

1 celery stalk, finely diced

2 medium tomatoes, finely chopped

2 cloves garlic, crushed

1 teaspoon sugar

4 cups beef stock

½ butternut squash, peeled, seeded, and diced

1 medium potato, peeled and diced

½ teaspoon ground turmeric

2 bay leaves

1 tablespoon coarsely chopped fresh coriander

2 tablespoons coarsely chopped fresh basil

2 tablespoons coarsely chopped fresh mint

1 cup plain yogurt

PREPARATION

1. Season the beef with the cumin, salt, and pepper. Heat the oil in a large pan over medium-high heat, until hot enough for frying. Brown the beef in batches, sautéing it on both sides to seal in the juices. Remove the beef from the pan using a slotted spoon, and set aside.

2. Using the same pan, heat the butter over medium heat until melted. Add the onion, leek, and celery, and sauté until tender.

3. Transfer the vegetables to a soup pot. Add the tomatoes, garlic, sugar, and stock, and bring to a boil.

4. Stir in the beef, squash, potato, turmeric, and bay leaves. Reduce heat, and simmer until the meat is tender, about 1 hour. Remove the bay leaves.

5. Stir in the coriander, basil, and mint. Remove from the heat, and set aside to cool. Stir in the yogurt.

6. Reheat gently over low heat before serving.

ENTRÉES

BAKED SALMON WITH MINT SAUCE

Salmon steaks are flavorful and juicy, but they cook quickly; be sure to keep your eye on them as they bake, so that they don't dry out.

INGREDIENTS

Serves 6

3 medium potatoes, peeled and sliced into rounds

1 tablespoon coriander seeds

2 cups plain yogurt

¼ cup fresh mint leaves

2 tablespoons freshly squeezed lemon juice

2 teaspoons freshly grated lemon zest

1 tablespoon olive oil

Salt

6 medium salmon steaks

Coarsely ground black pepper

PREPARATION

1. Place the potatoes in a large pot, and cover with salted water. Bring to a boil, and cook until soft, about 20 minutes. Drain and set aside.

2. Preheat the oven to 450°F.

3. Crush the coriander seeds with a mortar and pestle. Place the yogurt, mint, lemon juice, lemon zest, oil, crushed coriander seeds, and salt to taste in a food processor. Process until blended.

4. Lay the salmon steaks in a shallow baking dish. Top with potato slices and pour the yogurt mixture over top. Sprinkle with black pepper to taste.

5. Grill until the salmon is tender, about 13 minutes. Serve immediately.

VEGETABLE CURRY

*Served on a bed of steamed rice, this creamy curry makes a filling
vegetarian meal.*

INGREDIENTS

Serves 4

2 tablespoons canola oil

1 onion, sliced

2 cloves garlic, crushed

2 tablespoons red curry paste

2 cups vegetable stock

2 large sweet potatoes, peeled
and cubed

1 pound fresh green beans,
trimmed and halved

1 pound cherry tomatoes,
halved

1 cup cauliflower florets, cut
small

2 medium baby zucchini, sliced
into rounds

3 tablespoons freshly squeezed
lime juice

1 tablespoon soy sauce

1 teaspoon sugar

¼ cup coconut milk

¼ cup plain yogurt

Salt

¼ cup chopped fresh coriander

PREPARATION

1. Heat the oil in a large pot over
medium-high heat. Add the
onion and sauté for 2 minutes.
Add the garlic and sauté for
another minute. Add the curry
paste, reduce heat to medium,
and cook until fragrant.

2. Add the stock and sweet
potatoes and bring to a boil.
Reduce heat and simmer until
the potatoes are tender, about
15 minutes.

3. Add the green beans, cherry
tomatoes, cauliflower, and
zucchini. Simmer gently until the
vegetables are cooked. Stir in the
lime juice, soy sauce, and sugar,
and set aside to cool.

4. In a small mixing bowl, whisk
together the coconut milk and
yogurt. Pour into the soup, and
add salt to taste. Sprinkle with
coriander leaves.

5. Reheat gently on low heat
before serving.

ROTINI WITH BROCCOLI SAUCE

*The curly shape of rotini makes it perfect for holding plenty of sauce. Using
whole wheat noodles adds a rich, nutty flavor.*

INGREDIENTS

Serves 4

½ pound whole wheat rotini

2 cups broccoli florets

2 tablespoons olive oil

1 tablespoon butter

2 cloves garlic, crushed

½ teaspoon crushed red pepper
flakes

2 tablespoons chopped fresh
sage

2 tablespoons chopped fresh
basil

Pinch of sugar

Salt and coarsely ground black
pepper

¾ cup plain yogurt

1 tablespoon water

1 teaspoon freshly grated
lemon zest

¼ cup toasted pine nuts, for
garnish

PREPARATION

1. Bring a large pot of salted
water to a boil. Add the rotini
and cook according to the
instructions on the package.
Drain and set aside.

2. Bring a medium pot of salted
water to a boil. Add the broccoli
and blanch for about 5 minutes,
until tender. Drain and set aside.

3. Heat the oil and butter over
medium heat in a large saucepan.
Add the garlic, red pepper flakes,
sage, basil, sugar, and salt and
pepper to taste, and cook for
about 3 minutes. Stir in the rotini
and remove from the heat.

4. In a small mixing bowl, whisk
together the yogurt, water, and
lemon zest. Fold the mixture into
the rotini, then stir in the
broccoli.

5. Reheat gently on low heat
before serving. Garnish each
serving with a tablespoon of pine
nuts.

HAMBURGERS WITH CORIANDER SAUCE

Elevate hamburgers to new heights with this flavorful coriander sauce. Replace ground beef with ground turkey or chicken for a lighter option.

INGREDIENTS

Serves 4 to 6

Sauce:

1½ cups plain yogurt

2 tablespoons mayonnaise

3 cloves garlic, crushed

¾ cup fresh coriander

2 tablespoons olive oil

½ teaspoon salt

¼ teaspoon sugar

Hamburgers:

2 pounds ground beef

2 medium onions, finely diced

1 tablespoon finely chopped fresh basil

1 teaspoon cumin

1 teaspoon paprika

½ teaspoon nutmeg

1 tablespoon soy sauce

1 teaspoon crushed red pepper flakes

2 large free-range eggs, lightly whisked

¾ cup breadcrumbs

Olive oil, for brushing

PREPARATION

1. Place the yogurt, mayonnaise, garlic, coriander, oil, salt, and sugar in a food processor, and process until smooth.

2. Transfer to an airtight container, and refrigerate until ready to use.

3. Preheat the oven to 350°F.

4. Mix the beef, onions, basil, cumin, paprika, nutmeg, soy sauce, red pepper flakes, eggs, and breadcrumbs together in a large bowl, until thoroughly combined. Rub olive oil on hands, and shape the mixture into 3-inch patties.

5. Brush a baking sheet with olive oil. Arrange the patties on the sheet, and bake until the meat is tender, between 20 and 40 minutes, depending on how you like them.

6. Transfer the hamburgers to a serving dish, drizzle the sauce over them, and serve immediately.

SPICY CHICKEN WITH MINT SAUCE

Serve this chicken with Basmati rice and fresh Spinach Raita (page 28) for a tasty and traditional Indian meal.

INGREDIENTS

Serves 4 to 6

1 teaspoon ground turmeric

1 teaspoon ground cumin

2 cloves garlic, crushed

1 teaspoon garam masala

½ small red chili pepper, seeded and finely sliced

2 teaspoons sugar

¼ teaspoon ground cinnamon

1 tablespoon grated fresh ginger

2 tablespoons peanut oil

2 teaspoons sweet paprika

Salt

1½ pounds boneless, skinless chicken breast, cut into strips

¾ cup plain yogurt

½ cup fresh mint leaves

2 cups frozen peas, thawed

PREPARATION

1. In a large bowl, mix together the turmeric, cumin, garlic, garam masala, chili pepper, sugar, cinnamon, ginger, 1 tablespoon of the peanut oil, 1 teaspoon of the paprika, and salt to taste. Add the chicken and toss to coat. Cover with plastic wrap, and transfer to the refrigerator to marinate for at least 3 hours, or overnight.

2. To make the sauce, place the yogurt and mint in a food processor, and process until smooth. Cover, and refrigerate until ready to serve.

3. In a large frying pan or wok, heat the remaining tablespoon of peanut oil and teaspoon of paprika over medium heat. Add the chicken, and sauté in batches until cooked through, about 8 minutes for each batch. Mix the peas into the last batch of chicken, and cook until hot.

4. Transfer the chicken to a large serving dish. Drizzle the sauce on top, and serve warm.

GRILLED SOLE IN SPICY GINGER SAUCE

The seasoning in this sauce delicately brings out the flavor in the fish, without overpowering it.

INGREDIENTS

Serves 4 to 6

1 teaspoon garam masala

½ teaspoon nutmeg

3 cloves garlic, crushed

1 medium onion, chopped

1 tablespoon grated fresh ginger

1 teaspoon crushed red pepper flakes

2 teaspoons freshly squeezed lime juice

1¼ cups plain yogurt

Salt and freshly ground black pepper

Olive oil, for brushing

4 sole fillets

2 tablespoons chopped fresh coriander

Coriander sprigs, for garnish

PREPARATION

1. Place the garam masala, nutmeg, garlic, onion, ginger, and red pepper flakes in a food processor. Process until blended. Add the lime juice, yogurt, and salt and pepper to taste, and process until thick and creamy.

2. Brush a baking dish with olive oil. Rub the sole with olive oil and coriander on both sides, and place in the baking dish. Pour the yogurt mixture on top, cover with plastic wrap, and marinate in the refrigerator for about 20 minutes.

3. Preheat the oven to 450°F.

4. Grill the fish until tender, about 10 minutes. Garnish with coriander and serve.

LAMB IN CURRY SAUCE

*A staple meat in many parts of Europe, Africa, and the Middle East, lamb makes
a lovely alternative to beef or chicken. Serve this curry with boiled new potatoes.*

INGREDIENTS

Serves 4 to 6

1 tablespoon olive oil

1 tablespoon butter

2 small red onions, diced

1 tablespoon grated fresh ginger

2 cloves garlic, crushed

1 to 2 small red chili peppers, seeded and thinly sliced

¼ cup coarsely chopped fresh coriander

1 large tomato, chopped

1 teaspoon sugar

1 teaspoon salt

2 tablespoons chopped fresh mint

1 tablespoon freshly squeezed lime juice

1 cup vegetable or meat stock

2 tablespoons peanut oil

1 tablespoon soy sauce

2 pounds lamb stew meat, cut into 1½-inch cubes

1 cup plain yogurt

PREPARATION

1. Heat the olive oil and butter in a large pot, over medium-high heat. Add the onions, and sauté until tender. Mix in the ginger, garlic, chili peppers, coriander, tomato, sugar, salt, mint, lime juice, and stock. Bring to a boil, then reduce heat and simmer while you prepare the lamb.

2. Separately, heat the peanut oil and soy sauce in a large pan over medium-high heat. Cook the lamb in batches, turning the pieces regularly until brown on all sides, about 10 minutes per batch.

3. Add the lamb to the sauce, and continue cooking, covered, over low heat for about 30 minutes. Remove the lid, and cook for another 30 minutes, or until the lamb is soft.

4. Remove from the heat and set aside, uncovered, to cool. Mix in the yogurt, and reheat gently before serving.

SOLE WITH SPINACH AND LENTILS

The lentils in this sauce make this dish particularly satisfying. Use fresh spinach when available, or substitute frozen spinach if necessary.

INGREDIENTS

Serves 4

2 tablespoons olive oil

2 tablespoons butter

4 sole fillets

Salt

1 small onion, finely diced

1 cup canned green lentils, washed and drained

2 cups fresh spinach, finely chopped

1 tablespoon finely chopped fresh coriander

1 clove garlic, crushed

1 tablespoon grated fresh ginger

1 teaspoon ground cumin

½ teaspoon red pepper flakes

1 teaspoon freshly squeezed lemon juice

1 cup plain yogurt

1 teaspoon freshly grated lemon zest

PREPARATION

1. Preheat the oven to 350°F.

2. Heat 1 tablespoon of the oil and 1 tablespoon of the butter in a large pan over medium-high heat. Add the sole, and cook until it is white all over, about 8 minutes on each side. Sprinkle with salt and transfer to a shallow baking dish.

3. Reheat the juices in the pan, adding the remaining tablespoons of oil and butter if necessary. Add the onion, and sauté until glassy.

4. Mix in the lentils, spinach, coriander, garlic, ginger, cumin, red pepper flakes, lemon juice, and salt to taste, and simmer at medium heat until the spinach is soft and the liquid has evaporated.

5. Remove from the heat, and set aside to cool. Stir in the yogurt.

6. Pour the lentil mixture over the fish and sprinkle with lemon zest. Bake until the fish is tender, about 15 minutes.

SESAME MEATBALLS WITH HERB SAUCE

The meatballs in this dish are baked, so they have less fat then fried varieties. Adding toasted sesame seeds gives them texture and charm, making them a great finger food at any time of day.

INGREDIENTS

Serves 4 to 6

Meatballs:

Olive oil, for brushing

2 pounds ground beef

1 small onion, finely diced

2 clove garlic, crushed

1 tablespoon finely chopped fresh mint

1 teaspoon sea salt

1 teaspoon paprika

½ teaspoon ground allspice

Pinch of ground cinnamon

1 teaspoon ground cumin

¾ cup breadcrumbs

1 large free-range egg, beaten

½ cup toasted sesame seeds

Sauce:

2 cups plain yogurt

2 tablespoons finely chopped fresh mint

2 tablespoons finely chopped fresh coriander

2 tablespoons finely chopped fresh basil

2 cloves garlic, crushed

1 teaspoon olive oil

1 teaspoon freshly squeezed lemon juice

Salt and freshly ground black pepper

PREPARATION

1. Preheat the oven to 350˚F. Brush olive oil on a large baking sheet.

2. In a large bowl, mix together the beef, onion, garlic, mint, salt, paprika, allspice, cinnamon, cumin, breadcrumbs, egg, and sesame seeds, until well combined.

3. Shape the mixture into 1-inch meatballs, and arrange on the baking sheet. Cook until the juices run clear and the meatballs are brown on all sides, between 20 and 40 minutes, according to your taste.

4. In the meantime, place the yogurt, mint, coriander, basil, garlic, oil, lemon juice, and salt and pepper to taste in a food processor, and process until smooth. Transfer to an airtight container, and refrigerate until ready to serve.

5. Serve the meatballs warm, with sauce on the side for dipping.

COD IN TAHINI SAUCE

Tahini, a thick creamy sauce made from ground sesame seeds, is a natural partner for tangy yogurt. Make this dish with sea bass, sole, or any other mildly flavored white fish.

INGREDIENTS

Serves 6

2 tablespoons olive oil

1 tablespoon caraway seeds

1 teaspoon paprika

2 tablespoons freshly squeezed lemon juice

Salt

4 cod fillets

½ cup pure tahini

2 cloves garlic, chopped

¼ cup water

½ cup plain yogurt

PREPARATION

1. Preheat the oven to 350°F.

2. Heat the oil in a large frying pan over medium-high heat. Add the caraway seeds, paprika, 1 tablespoon of the lemon juice, and salt, and simmer at low heat for about 5 minutes.

3. Add the cod, and cook until it is white all over, about 8 minutes on each side. Transfer the fish to a shallow baking dish, and set aside.

4. Place the remaining tablespoon of lemon juice, tahini, garlic, water, and salt to taste in a food processor, and blend until creamy and smooth. Stir in the yogurt, mixing by hand until blended.

5. Pour the sauce over the fish, and bake until the fish is white on the inside and cooked through, about 10 to 15 minutes.

BEEF-STUFFED BABY EGGPLANTS

Eggplants are a dignified vegetable to begin with; stuffing them with beef, walnuts, and fresh mint elevates them to royal status.

INGREDIENTS

Serves 4 to 6

6 baby eggplants

1 tablespoon olive oil

1 small onion, finely diced

¼ cup finely chopped walnuts

1 pound ground beef

1 clove garlic, crushed

2 tablespoons plain yogurt

2 tablespoons finely chopped fresh mint

1 teaspoon ground cumin

1 teaspoon paprika

¾ cup breadcrumbs

2 large free-range eggs

Salt

Vegetable oil, for frying

Sauce:

2 cups plain yogurt

¼ cup fresh mint leaves

½ teaspoon salt

PREPARATION

1. Preheat the oven to 350°F. Cut the eggplants in half lengthwise, and hollow out the centers.

2. Heat the olive oil in a large pan over medium-high heat. Add the onion, and sauté until glassy. Mix in the walnuts, reduce heat, and cook until the onion is golden. Remove from heat, and set aside.

3. Mix together the beef, garlic, yogurt, mint, cumin, paprika, breadcrumbs, eggs, and salt to taste in a large bowl. Stir in the onion mixture until well combined.

4. Firmly press the beef mixture into the eggplant shells.

5. Heat 1 inch of vegetable oil in a large frying pan. Fry the eggplants in batches for about 4 minutes on each side, to seal.

6. Transfer the eggplants to a baking sheet, and bake until the meat is cooked through, about 40 minutes.

7. In the meantime, place the yogurt, mint, and salt in a blender, and blend until smooth. Refrigerate until ready to serve.

8. Transfer the eggplants to a serving dish, and drizzle the mint sauce on top, just before serving.

FISH CAKES WITH TARTAR SAUCE

This dish tastes just like the fare served at traditional pubs across the British Isles. Play a CD of your favorite English rock band to complete the effect.

INGREDIENTS

Serves 6

Sauce:

1 cup plain yogurt

1 tablespoon mayonnaise

2 teaspoons freshly grated lemon zest

2 teaspoons freshly squeezed lemon juice

2 tablespoons finely diced gherkins

2 tablespoons finely diced capers

1 tablespoon diced chives

1 small red chili pepper, seeded and finely chopped

Fish Cakes:

2 tablespoons vegetable oil, plus more for frying

1 large onion, finely diced

3 large carrots, peeled and grated

2 pounds whitefish, minced

1 teaspoon salt

1 tablespoon sugar

2 large free-range eggs

¾ cup breadcrumbs

Lemon wedges, for garnish

PREPARATION

1. Place the yogurt, mayonnaise, lemon zest, lemon juice, gherkins, capers, chives, and chili pepper in a medium bowl, and mix well. Refrigerate until ready to serve.

2. Heat 2 tablespoons of vegetable oil in a small saucepan over medium heat. Add the onion and carrots and sauté until golden. Set aside to cool, and then transfer to a large bowl.

3. Add the fish, salt, sugar, eggs, and breadcrumbs, and mix until combined. Shape the mixture into thick 2-inch patties.

4. Heat 1 inch of oil in a large skillet, over medium-high heat. Cook the patties in batches for about 4 or 5 minutes on each side, until crispy and golden. Transfer to a plate lined with a paper towel, to soak up any excess oil.

5. Serve the fish cakes warm, with tartar sauce and lemon wedges.

MEDITERRANEAN-STYLE SOLE WITH FETA CHEESE

This dish features a variety of flavors and complementary colors. Serve with some new potatoes for a light summer meal.

INGREDIENTS

Serves 4

1 cup crumbled feta cheese

1 cup plain yogurt

2 tablespoons olive oil

4 sole fillets

1 medium onion, finely chopped

Salt

2 large ripe tomatoes, diced

2 cloves garlic, crushed

1 teaspoon sugar

1 tablespoon finely chopped fresh basil

1 tablespoon finely chopped fresh oregano

1 tablespoon finely chopped fresh sage

Coarsely ground black pepper

PREPARATION

1. Preheat the oven to 450°F. Mix together the feta and yogurt, and set aside.

2. In a large frying pan, heat 1 tablespoon of the oil over medium-high heat. Add the sole and fry until white all around, about 8 minutes on each side. Transfer to a shallow baking dish.

3. Reheat the juices in the pan, adding the remaining tablespoon of olive oil if necessary. Add the onion and salt to taste, and sauté until glassy. Mix in the tomatoes, garlic, and sugar. Reduce the heat, and simmer for about 15 minutes.

4. Add the basil, oregano, and sage, and simmer for another 5 minutes.

5. Pour the tomato mixture over the fish. Spoon the feta mixture on top, and sprinkle with pepper. Grill for 10 to 15 minutes, until the fish is crispy on the outside and white on the inside.

GRILLED CHICKEN IN CUMIN MARINADE

Though the sauce in this dish is simple to make, the taste is complex and intriguing. Squeeze fresh lemon juice on top, to bring out the flavors, just before serving.

INGREDIENTS

Serves 6

2 tablespoons cumin seeds

1 small onion, coarsely chopped

5 cloves garlic, crushed

2 tablespoons coarsely chopped fresh coriander

1 tablespoon paprika

2 tablespoons freshly squeezed lemon juice

1 cup plain yogurt

12 chicken thighs

1 tablespoon olive oil

Salt and black pepper

Lemon wedges, for garnish

PREPARATION

1. Toast the cumin seeds in a dry pan over medium heat until aromatic, about 2 minutes.

2. Place the onion, garlic, coriander, paprika, and lemon juice in a food processor. Add the cumin seeds, and process until blended.

3. Add the yogurt, and process until blended.

4. Place the chicken in a shallow baking dish, and rub with olive oil, salt, and pepper.

5. Pour the yogurt mixture over the chicken. Cover with plastic wrap, and marinate in the refrigerator for 2 hours.

6. Preheat the oven to 450°F.

7. Grill the chicken for about 15 minutes, or until the juices run clear. Turn the chicken every few minutes as it grills, so that it doesn't burn. Garnish with lemon wedges before serving.

COD IN MUSTARD SAUCE

This tangy sauce goes well with a variety of white fish. I used cod, but you can use flounder, sole, or any other Catch of the Day.

INGREDIENTS

Serves 6

1 tablespoon olive oil

4 whole allspice

2 bay leaves

1 tablespoon Dijon-style mustard

A few whole peppercorns

5 sprigs fresh thyme

2 cloves garlic, crushed

¼ teaspoon sugar

Salt

2 cups plain yogurt

1 tablespoon butter, melted

6 cod fillets

PREPARATION

1. In a small pan, heat the oil over medium-high heat. Add the allspice, bay leaves, mustard, peppercorns, thyme, garlic, sugar, and salt to taste. Reduce heat to low, and cook until the spices are fragrant, about 5 minutes. Remove from heat, and set aside to cool.

2. Mix in the yogurt, and set aside for 20 minutes for the flavors to blend.

3. Preheat the oven to 350°F.

4. Brush butter on both sides of the fish. Sprinkle with salt, and place in a shallow baking dish.

5. Pour the sauce through a strainer and over the fish. Bake until the fish is cooked through and white on the inside, about 15 to 20 minutes.

BAKED
GOODS

ENERGY LOAF

Containing sesame seeds, pumpkin seeds, and sunflower seeds, this loaf is brimming with energy. Make a loaf the day before going on a picnic or long hike—it's a perfect snack during an active day!

INGREDIENTS

Makes 1 loaf

Natural cooking spray, for greasing

2 cups plain yogurt

3 tablespoons honey

2 cups whole wheat flour

1 cup wheat germ

½ cup crushed wheat

1 teaspoon salt

1 teaspoon baking soda

¼ cup sesame seeds

¼ cup pumpkin seeds

¼ cup poppy seeds

PREPARATION

1. Preheat the oven to 350°F. Grease a standard loaf pan with natural cooking spray.

2. Pour the yogurt and honey into a medium bowl, and beat with an electric beater.

3. In another bowl, mix together the flour, wheat germ, crushed wheat, salt, baking soda, sesame seeds, pumpkin seeds, and poppy seeds.

4. Add the flour mixture to the yogurt mixture, and mix until combined.

5. Transfer the dough to the loaf pan, and bake for 1 hour, or until a toothpick inserted in the center comes out clean.

6. Transfer to a wire rack to cool for 15 minutes. Turn the bread out onto the rack, and cool completely before serving.

CORNBREAD

This cornbread recipe has its own distinct charm, thanks to the addition of freshly creamed corn. It's a delicious twist on a traditional favorite.

INGREDIENTS

Makes 1 loaf

Natural cooking spray, for greasing

1 cup frozen corn

1½ cups yellow cornmeal

½ cup unbleached all-purpose flour

3 tablespoons sugar

1 tablespoon baking powder

½ teaspoon salt

¼ teaspoon black pepper

2 tablespoons salted butter

½ small onion, grated

1 cup plain yogurt

2 tablespoons vegetable oil

2 large free-range eggs, beaten

PREPARATION

1. Preheat the oven to 400°F. Grease a standard loaf pan with natural cooking spray, and line with parchment paper.

2. Heat a small pot of water to boiling, and add the frozen corn. Cook until just soft, about 4 minutes, and drain. Transfer to a food processor, and process until creamed.

3. Combine the cornmeal, flour, sugar, baking powder, salt, and pepper in a large bowl. Set aside.

4. Melt the butter in a small pan over medium heat. Add the onion, and sauté until just golden. Remove from heat, and set aside.

5. In another bowl, whisk together the yogurt, oil, and eggs. Add the onion to the yogurt mixture, and mix well.

6. Pour the yogurt mixture into the cornmeal mixture, and mix just until combined. Stir in the creamed corn.

7. Transfer the butter to the loaf pan, and bake for 45 minutes, or until a toothpick inserted in the center comes out clean.

8. Transfer to a wire rack, and cool before serving.

YOGURT SCONES

Serve these scones with fresh cream, marmalade, and a cup of strong tea for a typically British afternoon snack.

INGREDIENTS

Makes 12 scones

Natural cooking spray, for greasing

2 cups unbleached all-purpose flour

3 teaspoons baking powder

⅓ cup cold butter

1 large free-range egg, beaten

Pinch of salt

2 tablespoons sugar

1 cup plain yogurt

PREPARATION

1. Preheat the oven to 400°F. Grease a standard 12-cup muffin pan with natural cooking spray.

2. Sift together the flour and baking powder in a large mixing bowl.

3. Cut in the butter until the mixture resembles coarse meal.

4. Add the egg, salt, sugar, and yogurt, and mix just until combined.

5. Spoon the dough into the muffin cups, and bake for about 15 minutes.

6. Transfer the pan to a wire rack to cool for 5 minutes. Turn the scones out onto the rack to cool completely.

THREE-CHEESE MUSHROOM PIE

With feta, Parmesan, and ricotta cheeses, this cheesy pie is a delicious alternative to pizza. It's immeasurably more elegant, too.

INGREDIENTS

Makes one 10-inch pie

Crust:

Natural cooking spray, for greasing

2 cups unbleached all-purpose flour

1 teaspoon baking powder

½ cup grated cheddar cheese

¼ teaspoon sea salt

⅔ cup cold butter, cut into small cubes

½ cup light cream

Filling:

3 tablespoons dried porcini mushrooms

1 tablespoon butter

1 tablespoon olive oil

1 leek, finely diced

1 celery stalk, finely diced

Salt and black pepper

1 tablespoon chopped fresh mint

1 tablespoon chopped fresh basil

1 tablespoon dried sage

3 large egg yolks, lightly whisked

2 cups plain yogurt

1 cup crumbled feta cheese

¾ cup salted ricotta cheese

½ cup grated cheddar cheese

PREPARATION

1. Grease a 10-inch pie plate with natural cooking spray.

2. Place the flour, baking powder, cheddar cheese, salt, and butter in a food processor, and process until it resembles coarse meal. Transfer to a large mixing bowl and stir in the cream. Knead gently to form a ball.

3. Press the dough evenly into the pie plate. Cover with plastic wrap, and refrigerate for 1 hour.

4. In the meantime, place the mushrooms in a small bowl. Cover with boiling water, and allow to sit for 20 minutes. Drain well, finely chop, and set aside.

5. Preheat the oven to 350°F.

6. Melt the butter and olive oil in a small saucepan over medium heat. Add the leek, celery, and salt and pepper to taste, and sauté until the leek turns glassy.

7. Mix in the mushrooms and sauté for 2 minutes. Remove from the heat, and set aside to cool.

8. Add the mint, basil, sage, egg yolks, yogurt, and cheeses, and mix thoroughly.

9. Pour the filling into the pie shell, and bake for 40 minutes, or until the filling is firm and the pastry is golden.

POPPY SEED BREAD

Because this recipe doesn't require yeast, this bread takes much less time to prepare than regular bread.

INGREDIENTS

Makes 2 loaves

Natural cooking spray, for greasing

2 cups unbleached all-purpose flour

1 cup whole wheat flour

1 teaspoon salt

1 teaspoon baking powder

1 teaspoon baking soda

½ cup poppy seeds

3 large free-range eggs

1 cup vegetable oil

1 cup light brown sugar

2 cups plain yogurt

1 tablespoon freshly squeezed lemon juice

2 tablespoons crushed walnuts

PREPARATION

1. Preheat the oven to 325°F. Grease 2 standard loaf pans with natural cooking spray.

2. Sift together the flours, salt, baking powder, and baking soda in a large bowl. Mix in the poppy seeds.

3. In another bowl, beat the eggs. Stir in the oil and light brown sugar, and beat until creamy. Add the yogurt and lemon juice, and stir until blended.

4. Fold the flour mixture into the yogurt mixture, and mix just until combined.

5. Spoon the batter into the loaf pans. Sprinkle the walnuts on top, pressing down lightly so that they sit firmly on the surface.

6. Bake for 1 hour, or until a toothpick inserted in the center comes out clean. If the loaves start to brown too early, cover with foil after 40 minutes.

7. Transfer the loaf pans to a wire rack, and cool about 10 minutes. Turn the loaves out onto the rack to cool completely before slicing.

CHERRY TOMATO AND BASIL TART

When cherry tomatoes are in season, this is the perfect dish for celebrating them.
Try preparing this tart in a square pan, to create a pleasing contrast with the
round shape of the tomatoes.

INGREDIENTS

Makes one 9-inch square tart

Natural cooking spray, for greasing

1 sheet frozen shortcrust pastry, thawed

All-purpose flour, for dusting

2 tablespoons olive oil

1 small onion, thinly sliced lengthwise

1 pound cherry tomatoes, sliced in half lengthwise

1 tablespoon balsamic vinegar

1 tablespoon light brown sugar

Sea salt

2 cups plain yogurt

2 egg yolks

½ cup coarsely chopped fresh basil

8 ounces feta cheese, cut into ¼-inch cubes

Coarsely ground black pepper

PREPARATION

1. Preheat the oven to 350°F. Grease a 9-inch square tart pan with natural cooking spray.

2. Roll out the pastry on a lightly floured surface, until it is ¼-inch thick. Press into the tart pan, and bake for 15 minutes, or until golden. Transfer to a wire rack to cool.

3. Heat 1 tablespoon of the olive oil in a small pan. Add the onion, and sauté until slightly golden. Remove from heat.

4. Place the cherry tomatoes, vinegar, and light brown sugar in a shallow baking dish. Sprinkle with salt, and marinate for 20 minutes.

5. Whisk together the yogurt, egg yolks, and basil in a medium bowl. Add the feta, onion, and cherry tomatoes, and mix until combined.

6. Pour the filling into the pie shell. Sprinkle pepper on top, and bake at 350°F for 45 minutes, until the filling is firm and the pastry is golden.

MINI WALNUT AND BEEF PIES

These miniature pies have a nutty flavor and crunchy texture. Serve with a side dish of mashed potatoes, for a stylish yet substantial lunch.

INGREDIENTS

Makes 10 mini pies

Natural cooking spray, for greasing

5 tablespoons vegetable oil

1 medium onion, finely diced

2 tablespoons chopped fresh parsley

2 tablespoons chopped fresh coriander

1 tablespoon ground cumin

1 tablespoon paprika

1 teaspoon nutmeg

2 cloves garlic, crushed

½ cup finely chopped walnuts

Salt and black pepper

¾ cup plain yogurt

3 teaspoons natural soy sauce

1½ pounds rump steak, cubed small

1 sheet frozen puff pastry, thawed

All-purpose flour, for dusting

PREPARATION

1. Preheat the oven to 350°F. Spray ten 3-inch pie plates with natural cooking spray.

2. Heat 2 tablespoons of oil in a large pan, over medium heat. Add the onion, parsley, coriander, cumin, paprika, and nutmeg, and cook for about 5 minutes.

3. Reduce heat and mix in the garlic, walnuts, and salt and pepper to taste. Simmer for about 10 minutes. Remove from heat, and set aside to cool.

4. Transfer to a large bowl, mix in the yogurt, and set aside.

5. Heat a tablespoon of oil and a teaspoon of soy sauce in a large saucepan over medium heat. Cook the beef in batches, adding oil and soy sauce as necessary, until it is tender and brown on all sides.

6. Stir the beef into the yogurt mixture, and cover with plastic wrap. Transfer to the refrigerator, and marinate for 20 minutes.

7. In the meantime, roll out the puff pastry on a lightly floured surface, until it is ¼ inch thick. Divide the pastry into 10 equal pieces, and press a piece into each of the pie plates.

8. Spoon the filling into the pie shells, and bake for 40 minutes, or until the pastry is golden.

CURRIED POLENTA AND SPINACH BAKE

Creamy polenta, a staple in many European and South American countries, is adept at taking on flavors. Serve this dish with a fresh leafy salad for a hearty supper.

INGREDIENTS

Serves 6

3 cups fresh spinach leaves, trimmed

1 tablespoon peanut oil

3 tablespoons butter

1 onion, finely chopped

¼ cup finely chopped fresh coriander

Salt

2 cloves garlic, crushed

½ teaspoon ground cumin

¼ teaspoon ground turmeric

½ teaspoon ground ginger

½ teaspoon red chili powder

1 cup crumbled feta cheese

1 cup plain yogurt

¼ teaspoon ground nutmeg

¼ teaspoon ground cinnamon

1 tablespoon light brown sugar

1 tablespoon freshly grated orange zest

2 cups canned pumpkin

Olive oil, for brushing

4 cups vegetable or chicken stock

2 cups milk

2 cups polenta

¼ cup freshly grated Parmesan cheese

Freshly ground black pepper

PREPARATION

1. Bring a pot of salted water to a boil. Add the spinach, and blanch for 4 minutes. Drain the spinach, squeeze out the excess water, and set aside.

2. Heat the peanut oil and 1 tablespoon of the butter in a saucepan over medium heat. Stir in the onion, coriander, and salt to taste. Cook for about 8 minutes.

3. Mix in the spinach, garlic, cumin, turmeric, ginger, and chili powder. Reduce heat, cover, and simmer for 5 minutes.

4. Stir in the feta, add black pepper according to taste, and remove from heat. Set aside uncovered to cool. Stir in the yogurt.

(continued on page 92)

(continued from page 90)

5. Melt 1 tablespoon of the butter in a small pan over low heat. Add the nutmeg, cinnamon, light brown sugar, and orange zest, and cook while stirring, until the light brown sugar has dissolved.

6. Mix in the pumpkin, and remove from heat.

7. Preheat the oven to 350°F. Brush a 2-quart casserole dish with olive oil.

8. Pour the stock into a large pot, and bring to a boil over medium heat. Add the milk, and heat for a few minutes.

9. Slowly pour in the polenta, while stirring constantly. After all the polenta has been added, reduce heat and continue stirring. Simmer until all the liquid evaporates.

10. Remove from heat. Stir in the Parmesan cheese and the remaining tablespoon of butter.

11. Spread half of the polenta mixture in the casserole dish. Layer with the spinach mixture, then the pumpkin mixture. Top with the rest of the polenta mixture, and brush with olive oil.

12. Bake for 20 minutes, or until golden and crispy. Remove from the oven, and cool slightly before serving.

LEEK AND BRIE PIE

A close relation to onions and garlic, leeks have a much more delicate and subtle flavor. Sautéing the leeks gently in melted butter really brings out their sweetness.

INGREDIENTS

Serves 6

Crust:

Natural cooking spray, for greasing

4 medium sweet potatoes, peeled and cubed

1 tablespoon butter, melted

2 large free-range eggs, whisked lightly

¾ cup breadcrumbs

1 tablespoon finely chopped fresh dill

1 teaspoon baking powder

Sea salt

Filling:

1 tablespoon butter

4 small leeks, finely diced

2 teaspoons light brown sugar

6 ounces Brie cheese, coarsely chopped

⅓ cup plain yogurt

2 large free-range eggs, beaten lightly

¼ teaspoon ground nutmeg

¼ teaspoon dried sage

Salt and black pepper

PREPARATION

1. Grease a 10-inch pie plate with natural cooking spray.

2. Cover the sweet potatoes with cold water, and bring to a boil. Reduce heat, and cook for 15 minutes, or until tender. Drain.

3. Place the sweet potatoes, butter, eggs, breadcrumbs, dill, baking powder, and salt to taste in a food processor, and process until blended. Press the mixture into the pie plate, and refrigerate for 20 minutes. Preheat the oven to 350°F.

4. Transfer the pie shell to the oven, and bake until slightly golden, about 20 minutes. Transfer to a wire rack to cool.

5. Melt the butter in a pan over low heat. Add the leeks, and cook while stirring for 15 minutes, until tender.

6. Add the light brown sugar, and continue to cook while stirring, until the leeks caramelize. Remove from the heat, and stir in the Brie.

7. In a large bowl, combine the yogurt, eggs, nutmeg, sage, and salt and pepper to taste.

8. Spread the leek mixture evenly on the bottom of the pie shell. Pour the yogurt mixture on top, and bake for 20 minutes, until the filling is firm and the pastry is golden.

CAKES
AND
DESSERTS

PEACH CAKE WITH PISTACHIO TOPPING

With its cool white frosting and textured pistachio topping, this cake has a magnificent presence. Serve on an antique-style cake plate to maximize its elegant appearance.

INGREDIENTS

Serves 10 to 12

Cake:

Natural cooking spray, for greasing

1 cup unsalted butter, softened

1 cup sugar

1 teaspoon pure vanilla extract

3 large free-range eggs

2½ cups self-rising flour, sifted

2 tablespoons milk

1 cup plain yogurt

1 pound small firm peaches, peeled, cored, and chopped

Frosting:

⅓ cup whipping cream

1 cup confectioner's sugar

½ teaspoon pure vanilla extract

½ cup crushed pistachios

PREPARATION

1. Preheat the oven to 325°F. Grease a 9-inch springform pan with natural cooking spray, and line with parchment paper.

2. Cream the butter and sugar in an electric mixer, until smooth. Mix in the vanilla, and add the eggs one at a time, beating well between each egg.

3. Add the flour, milk, and yogurt in batches, while mixing at low speed.

4. Gently fold in the peaches with a rubber spatula, just until combined.

5. Pour the mixture into the pan, and bake for 1½ hours, or until golden. If the cake browns too quickly, cover with foil for the last 20 minutes of baking. Transfer to a wire rack, and cool for 10 minutes. Turn out the cake onto the rack, and cool completely before frosting.

6. To make the frosting, whisk together the cream, confectioner's sugar, and vanilla, until smooth. Pour frosting over the entire cake, allowing it to drip down the sides a little. Scatter pistachios on the top, and refrigerate until ready to serve.

MINI CHOCOLATE CAKES WITH WHIPPED YOGURT

This dessert is an elegant alternative to traditional chocolate cake. Serve with fresh berries for a light yet satisfying treat.

INGREDIENTS

Makes 12 mini cakes

Cream:

½ cup plain yogurt

½ cup whipping cream

Cake:

Natural cooking spray, for greasing

2 cups unbleached all-purpose flour

⅔ cup unsweetened cocoa powder

1½ teaspoons baking soda

½ cup butter, softened

1½ cups sugar

2 large free-range eggs

1½ cups plain yogurt

1 teaspoon pure vanilla extract

½ cup confectioner's sugar

PREPARATION

1. Whip together the yogurt and cream with an electric mixer, until light and fluffy. Transfer to an airtight container, and refrigerate until ready to serve.

2. Preheat the oven to 350°F. Grease a standard 12-cup muffin pan with natural cooking spray.

3. Sift together the flour, cocoa, and baking soda in a medium bowl.

4. Separately, cream together the butter and sugar in an electric mixer. Beat in the eggs one at a time.

5. Mix in the yogurt and the flour, alternately, in three parts. Take care not to mix too much. Stir in the vanilla.

6. Pour the batter into the muffin cups, and bake for about 30 minutes, or until a toothpick inserted in the center comes out clean.

7. Remove from the oven, and set on a wire rack to cool for about 10 minutes. Turn the cakes out onto the rack, and cool completely.

8. Sift confectioner's sugar on top of the cakes before serving, and serve with the chilled yogurt cream.

GINGER CHEESECAKE

Spice up a conventional cheesecake by using ginger cookies for the crust and adding fresh ginger juice to the filling.

INGREDIENTS

Serves 10 to 12

Crust:

Natural cooking spray, for greasing

1 cup finely ground ginger cookies

¼ cup ground almonds

⅓ cup unsalted butter, melted

Filling:

3 teaspoons grated fresh ginger

24 ounces light cream cheese

¾ cup plain yogurt

¾ cup sugar

4 large free-range eggs

1 tablespoon candied ginger, grated

1 teaspoon freshly grated lime zest

2 teaspoons freshly squeezed lime juice

2 egg whites

PREPARATION

1. Preheat the oven to 300°F, and place the rack in the bottom of the oven. Grease a 9-inch springform pan with natural cooking spray, and line with parchment paper.

2. Mix together the cookies, almonds, and butter. Press the mixture into the bottom of the pan, and refrigerate until ready to use.

3. Put a fine sieve over a small bowl, and place the ginger in the sieve. Press down on the ginger with a spoon, to release the juice. Set aside the juice, and discard the solids.

4. Combine the cream cheese, yogurt, and sugar in a large bowl, and mix together until light and fluffy. Add the eggs one at a time, beating well after each egg. Add the ginger juice, candied ginger, lime zest, and lime juice, and mix well.

5. Beat the egg whites in an electric mixer, until stiff peaks form.

6. Gently fold the egg whites into the yogurt mixture, until just combined.

7. Pour the filling into the crust, and bake for 1 hour and 10 minutes. Turn off the oven, open the door, and let the cake cool inside the oven for about 30 minutes. Transfer to a wire rack and cool completely. Cover with plastic wrap, and refrigerate overnight before serving.

YOGURT WITH CRANBERRY SYRUP

This attractive dessert makes a lovely finish to a festive meal.

INGREDIENTS

Serves 4

1 teaspoon butter

1 cup dried cranberries

¼ cup sugar

¼ cup pure apple juice

1 tablespoon orange zest

2 cups plain yogurt

1 tablespoon finely diced orange peel, for garnish

¼ cup dried cranberries for topping

PREPARATION

1. Place the butter in a saucepan, and melt over medium heat. Stir in the cranberries, and reduce heat to low. Add the sugar and apple juice, and simmer until the sugar has dissolved.

2. Remove from heat, stir in the orange zest, and set aside to cool.

3. Divide 1 cup of the yogurt between 4 individual serving dishes or stem glasses. Top with half of the cranberry mixture. Layer with the rest of the yogurt, and top each serving with a spoonful of cranberries. Sprinkle a little orange peel on top, and serve immediately.

PANNA COTTA WITH PASSION FRUIT SYRUP

This classic Italian dessert is elegant, impressive, and deceptively easy to make.
Serve with fresh espresso for a grand finale to any meal.

INGREDIENTS

Serves 8

Panna Cotta:

1 cup milk

1 tablespoon unflavored gelatin

1 teaspoon pure vanilla extract

2 teaspoons freshly grated lemon zest

2 cups heavy cream

1 cup plain yogurt

¼ cup superfine sugar

Pinch of salt

1 tablespoon freshly squeezed lemon juice

Sauce:

6 fresh passion fruit, halved

¼ cup superfine sugar

PREPARATION

1. Pour the milk into a nonstick saucepan. Sprinkle in the gelatin, and allow to sit for about 5 minutes to soften.

2. Add the vanilla and lemon zest, and heat over low-medium heat, until the gelatin dissolves. Whisk in the cream, yogurt, sugar, and salt, and cook for another 2 minutes, until the sugar has dissolved.

3. Remove from the heat and stir in the lemon juice.

4. Pour the cream mixture into eight ½-cup ramekins. Cover, and refrigerate for at least 6 hours, or until set.

5. To make the sauce, scoop out the flesh from the passion fruit. Place in a saucepan, and heat over low-medium heat. Whisk in the sugar until a syrup is formed. Remove from the heat and set aside to cool.

6. Remove the panna cotta from the refrigerator, just before serving. Fill a small pot with boiling water, and dip the bottom of the ramekins in the water, one at a time, for about 20 seconds. Invert the ramekin onto a plate, and tap lightly on the bottom to loosen.

7. Drizzle the syrup on top, and serve immediately.

APPLES AND SPICE YOGURT

Few things smell quite as comforting as apples, cloves, and cinnamon, gently cooking on the stove.

INGREDIENTS

Serves 4

1 teaspoon butter

2 medium red apples, peeled, cored, and diced

¼ teaspoon ground cinnamon

¼ teaspoon ground ginger

3 whole cloves

2 tablespoons pure apple juice

¼ teaspoon pure vanilla extract

2 cups plain yogurt

2 tablespoons chopped roasted almonds

1 tablespoon raw honey

PREPARATION

1. Heat the butter in a saucepan over medium heat. Add the apples, cinnamon, ginger, and cloves, and cook gently for about 5 minutes.

2. Mix in the apple juice and vanilla, and reduce heat to low. Continue cooking while stirring, until the apples are tender.

3. Remove the cloves and set aside to cool.

4. Put the yogurt into a glass bowl. Add the apples, sprinkle with the almonds, and drizzle honey on top.

5. Cover with plastic wrap, and refrigerate for 20 minutes, or until ready to serve.

COCONUT AND DATE YOGURT

*The dates in this dessert are cooked slowly, bringing out their natural sugar,
and making this an ideal dessert for diners with a sweet tooth.*

INGREDIENTS

Serves 4

1 teaspoon butter

1 cup dates, pitted and chopped

1 teaspoon light brown sugar

1 teaspoon ground cinnamon

¼ cup flaked unsweetened coconut

3 tablespoons milk

2 cups plain yogurt

3 tablespoons honey

PREPARATION

1. Heat the butter in a saucepan over medium heat. Add the dates, light brown sugar, and cinnamon, and cook over low heat for about 10 minutes. Remove from heat, and set aside to cool.

2. Place 2 tablespoons of the coconut in a dry saucepan, and toast over high heat until golden. Set aside.

3. Pour the milk into a small bowl. Add the remaining 2 tablespoons of coconut, and allow to soak for about 10 minutes. Whisk in the yogurt and 2 tablespoons of the honey.

4. Divide the date mixture among 4 individual dessert dishes. Pour the yogurt mixture on top, and sprinkle with toasted coconut. Cover with plastic wrap, and refrigerate until ready to serve.

5. Drizzle the remaining tablespoon of honey on top just before serving.

MIXED BERRY DESSERT

*Simple and sophisticated, this light dessert is a perfect finish to a filling meal.
Because it uses frozen berries, it's in season all year long!*

INGREDIENTS

Serves 8

2½ cups frozen mixed berries

1 cup plain yogurt

1 cup sugar

1 tablespoon freshly squeezed
lemon juice

¼ teaspoon pure vanilla extract

PREPARATION

1. Remove the berries from the
freezer, and allow to stand at
room temperature for about
15 minutes. Place in a food
processor, and process into finely
shaved ice.

2. Add the yogurt, sugar, lemon,
and vanilla, and mix until smooth.

3. Transfer to a glass bowl, and
serve immediately.

MANGO AND GINGER FROZEN YOGURT

Frozen yogurt is an excellent low-fat alternative to regular ice cream. This recipe produces a yogurt with a distinct sweet-spicy flavor.

INGREDIENTS

Serves 4

2 tablespoons grated fresh ginger

2 mangoes, peeled and cubed

½ cup sugar

2 tablespoons raw honey

½ cup milk

1 cup plain yogurt

¼ teaspoon peppermint extract

PREPARATION

1. Put a fine sieve over a small bowl, and place the ginger in the sieve. Press down on the ginger with a spoon, to release the juice. Set aside the juice, and discard the solids.

2. Place the mangoes, sugar, honey, and ginger juice in a food processor, and purée until smooth.

3. Stir in the milk, yogurt, and peppermint. Mix until combined, and freeze for at least 6 hours before serving.

PEAR AND HONEY FROZEN POPS

Who says frozen pops are just for kids? Use glass tumblers instead of traditional pop molds to add a touch of sophistication to this dessert.

INGREDIENTS

Serves 5

1 teaspoon butter

6 small Bosc pears, peeled, cored, and sliced

2 tablespoons light brown sugar

½ teaspoon pure vanilla extract

¼ cup raw honey

¾ cup plain yogurt

PREPARATION

1. Place the butter in a saucepan, and melt over medium heat. Add the pears, light brown sugar, and vanilla, and cook until the sugar has dissolved, about 8 minutes.

2. Reduce heat, and gently stir in the honey. Simmer at a low heat until the pears are cooked, about 10 minutes. Remove from the heat, and set aside to cool.

3. Place the pears and the yogurt in a food processor, and blend until smooth.

4. Transfer the mixture to thick glass tumblers or individual ice-pop molds. Insert wooden pop sticks, and freeze for at least 6 hours before serving.

YOGURT WITH SAUTÉED FIGS AND HONEY

There's nothing quite as luscious as fresh figs in season. The caramelizing process in this dish brings out their natural sweetness.

INGREDIENTS

Serves 4

1 teaspoon butter

4 plump fresh figs, sliced into rounds

2 tablespoons sugar

1 tablespoon pure apple juice

2 cups plain yogurt

1 tablespoon honey

PREPARATION

1. Heat the butter in a small saucepan over medium heat. Add the figs and sugar, reduce heat to low, and cook for about 5 minutes.

2. Add the apple juice, and continue cooking until the figs have caramelized. Remove from the heat and set aside to cool.

3. Pour the yogurt into a glass bowl. Top with the figs, and drizzle honey over the figs. Cover with plastic wrap, and refrigerate until ready to serve.

CARAMELIZED PEARS WITH MINT

The combination of flavors in this dessert is subtle and refreshing. As a perfect accompaniment, use extra mint leaves to make a refreshing cup of tea.

INGREDIENTS

Serves 4

1 teaspoon butter

4 medium Bosc pears, peeled, cored, and sliced

¼ teaspoon pure vanilla extract

3 star anise pods

¼ cup sugar

1 tablespoon finely chopped fresh mint

2 cups plain yogurt

1 tablespoon honey

PREPARATION

1. Heat the butter in a saucepan, over medium heat. Stir in the pears, vanilla, star anise pods, and sugar. Reduce heat to low, and cook gently until the pears are tender, about 10 minutes.

2. Remove from heat, take out the star anise pods, and set aside to cool.

3. Transfer the pears to a glass bowl, and stir in the mint. Pour the yogurt on top, and drizzle honey over it. Cover with plastic wrap, and refrigerate for 20 minutes, or until ready to serve.

YOGURT WITH BANANAS, DATES, AND ALMONDS

This dessert includes orange-flower water, a flavorful essence distilled from fresh orange blossoms.

INGREDIENTS

Serves 4

4 ripe bananas, peeled and sliced

1 cup pitted and chopped dates

3 cups plain yogurt

2 teaspoons orange-flower water

2 tablespoons flaked almonds, toasted

PREPARATION

1. Mix together the bananas and dates in a medium bowl.

2. Separately, mix together the yogurt and orange-flower water until blended.

3. Pour the banana mixture over the yogurt mixture, and sprinkle the almonds on top.

4. Cover with plastic wrap, and refrigerate until ready to serve.

YOGURT FIG MUFFINS

Morsels of dried figs make a deliciously sweet surprise in these muffins. Alternately, use juicy dates or plump raisins.

INGREDIENTS

Makes 12 muffins

2½ cups self-rising flour

¾ cup light brown sugar

1 large free-range egg, lightly beaten

1 teaspoon pure vanilla extract

⅔ cup vegetable oil

¾ cup plain yogurt

1½ cups chopped dried figs

PREPARATION

1. Preheat the oven to 400°F. Line a standard 12-cup muffin pan with paper liners.

2. Sift together the flour and light brown sugar in a large mixing bowl.

3. Mix in the egg, vanilla, oil, yogurt, and figs. Be careful not to mix too much, as the batter should be a bit lumpy.

4. Spoon the batter into the muffin cups, and bake for about 20 minutes, or until a toothpick inserted in the muffin center comes out clean.

5. Transfer the pan to a wire rack to cool for 5 minutes. Turn the muffins out onto the rack to cool completely.

BEVERAGES

APRICOT AND CARDAMOM SMOOTHIE

The cardamom in this recipe gives it an unmistakable flavor. Serve with lokum for a lovely Mediterranean treat.

INGREDIENTS

Serves 4

1 cup dried apricots

3 cups plain yogurt

2 tablespoons raw honey

1 teaspoon sugar

1 teaspoon ground cardamom

PREPARATION

1. Cover the apricots with boiling water, and allow to sit for 10 minutes, to soften. Drain and set aside.

2. Place the yogurt, honey, sugar, and cardamom in a food processor. Add the apricots and purée until smooth.

3. Transfer to an airtight container and refrigerate until ready to serve.

APPLE, MINT, AND GINGER SMOOTHIE

This smoothie is a great way to start your day. With fresh mint, juicy ginger, and crisp apples, it puts a natural bounce in your step!

INGREDIENTS

Serves 4

2 teaspoons grated fresh ginger

2 cups plain yogurt

2 tablespoons raw honey

2 red apples, peeled, cored, and diced

1 tablespoon chopped fresh mint

PREPARATION

1. Put a fine sieve over a small bowl, and place the ginger in the sieve. Press down on the ginger with a spoon to release the juice. Set aside the juice, and discard the solids.

2. Place the ginger juice, yogurt, honey, apples, and mint in a food processor. Purée until smooth.

3. Transfer to an airtight container and refrigerate until ready to serve.

CUCUMBER AND MINT SMOOTHIE

Ideal for people who prefer salty beverages to sweet ones, this smoothie is light and refreshing.

INGREDIENTS

Serves 4

3 cups plain yogurt

1 medium English cucumber, peeled and diced

2 tablespoons chopped fresh mint

Pinch of salt

Pinch of sugar

PREPARATION

1. Place the yogurt, cucumber, mint, salt, and sugar in a food processor. Purée until smooth.

2. Transfer to an airtight container, and refrigerate until ready to serve.

BANANA, HONEY, AND ALMOND SMOOTHIE

Sweet, spicy, and satisfying, this smoothie is perfect for relieving mid-afternoon hunger pains. It provides just enough energy to tide you over until dinner.

INGREDIENTS

Serves 4

3 cups plain yogurt

1 teaspoon ground nutmeg

2 tablespoons raw honey

2 tablespoons chopped roasted almonds, plus more for garnish

2 large ripe bananas, chopped

PREPARATION

1. Place the yogurt, nutmeg, honey, almonds, and bananas in a food processor. Purée until smooth.

2. Transfer to an airtight container, and refrigerate until ready to serve. Garnish with roasted almonds just before serving.

STRAWBERRY AND MINT SMOOTHIE

When strawberries are in season, it's a shame not to eat them at every opportunity! Using fresh mint in this smoothie really brings out the flavor of the berries.

INGREDIENTS

Serves 4

3 cups plain yogurt

1 cup fresh strawberries, washed and hulled

1 tablespoon raw honey

1 tablespoon chopped fresh mint

1 teaspoon pure vanilla extract

PREPARATION

1. Place the yogurt, strawberries, honey, mint, and vanilla in a food processor, and blend until smooth.

2. Transfer to an airtight container, and refrigerate until ready to serve. Serve chilled.

PINEAPPLE, LIME, AND GINGER SMOOTHIE

For a distinctly tropical taste, garnish this sunny smoothie with a few chunks of fresh pineapple.

INGREDIENTS

Serves 4

2 teaspoons grated fresh ginger

3 cups plain yogurt

½ fresh pineapple, peeled, cored, and diced

1½ tablespoons raw honey

1 teaspoon lime zest

1 teaspoon freshly squeezed lime juice

PREPARATION

1. Put a fine sieve over a small bowl and place the ginger in the sieve. Press down on the ginger with a spoon, to release the juice. Transfer the juice to a blender, and discard the solids.

2. Add the yogurt, pineapple, honey, lime zest, and lime juice, and blend until smooth.

3. Transfer to an airtight container, and refrigerate until ready to serve.

MANGO LASSI

When mangoes are in season, this is a great way of turning them into a refreshingly frothy beverage.

INGREDIENTS

Serves 2

1 mango, peeled and diced

2 cups plain yogurt

½ teaspoon grated fresh ginger

2 tablespoons sugar

2 tablespoons chopped fresh mint

4 ice cubes

PREPARATION

1. Place the mango, yogurt, ginger, sugar, mint, and ice cubes in a blender, and blend until smooth.

2. Pour into tall glasses, and serve immediately.

STRAWBERRY AND GINGER LASSI

Fresh strawberries give this lassi a natural sweetness that is subtle and aromatic.

INGREDIENTS

Serves 2

1 cup fresh strawberries, washed and hulled

2 cup plain yogurt

½ teaspoon grated fresh ginger

2 tablespoons sugar

1½ teaspoons rosewater

4 ice cubes

PREPARATION

1. Place the strawberries, yogurt, ginger, sugar, rosewater, and ice cubes in a blender, and blend until smooth.

2. Pour into tall glasses, and serve immediately.

ROSEWATER LASSI

Simple and aromatic, this traditional Indian beverage is perfect for cooling your palate on a hot day.

INGREDIENTS

Serves 2

2 cups plain yogurt

2 tablespoons rosewater

½ cup light brown sugar

4 ice cubes

PREPARATION

1. Place the yogurt, rosewater, light brown sugar, and ice cubes in a blender. Blend until smooth.

2. Pour into tall glasses, and serve immediately.

SAVORY LASSI

People who dream of traveling to India can indulge in one of its favorite drinks with this refreshingly spicy concoction.

INGREDIENTS

Serves 2

1 cup plain yogurt

½ cup water

½ cup milk

½ teaspoon salt

½ teaspoon garam masala

¼ teaspoon sugar

PREPARATION

1. Place the yogurt, water, milk, salt, garam masala, and sugar in a blender, and blend until smooth.

2. Pour into tall glasses and serve immediately.

BANANA AND STRAWBERRY SMOOTHIE

This creamy smoothie bears an uncanny resemblance to a traditional strawberry milkshake—only it has fewer calories, and much less fat.

INGREDIENTS

Serves 4

2 ripe bananas, frozen

2 cups fresh strawberries, washed and hulled

1 cup plain yogurt

1 cup milk

¼ cup raw honey

PREPARATION

1. Thaw the bananas at room temperature for about 10 minutes, or until they can be cut with a knife. Cut into large chunks and place in a blender.

2. Add the strawberries, yogurt, milk, and honey, and blend until smooth.

3. Serve immediately.